Tricky Troll

The Laidlaw Reading Program LEVEL 7

William Eller
Kathleen B. Hester

S. Elizabeth Davis

Thomas J. Edwards

Roger Farr

Jack W. Humphrey

DayAnn McClenathan

Nancy Lee Roser

Elizabeth M. Ryan

Ann Myra Seaver

Marian Alice Simmons

Margaret Wittrig

Patricia J. Cianciolo, *Children's literature*

David W. Reed, *Linguistics*

LAIDLAW BROTHERS • PUBLISHERS
A Division of Doubleday & Company, Inc.

RIVER FOREST, ILLINOIS

Irvine, California   Chamblee, Georgia   Dallas, Texas   Toronto, Canada

Acknowledgments

Atheneum Publishers, Inc., for the poems *A Lazy Thought* and *Wishing* by Eve Merriam from THERE IS NO RHYME FOR SILVER. Copyright © 1962 by Eve Merriam. From THERE IS NO RHYME FOR SILVER. Used by permission of Atheneum Publishers.

Chicago Zoological Society for helpful information for "A Job in the Sky."

Thomas Y. Crowell Company, Inc., for the poem "Cat Bath" by Aileen Fisher. From FEATHERED ONES AND FURRY by Aileen Fisher, Copyright © 1971 by Aileen Fisher. With permission of the publisher, Thomas Y. Crowell Company, Inc.

Thomas Y. Crowell Company, Inc., for "A Pet in a Bowl." Adapted from *The Rice Bowl Pet* by Patricia Miles Martin. Text copyright © 1962 by Patricia Miles Martin. Reprinted by permission of Thomas Y. Crowell Company, Inc., Publishers.

Follett Publishing Company for "The Dog Who Came to Dinner." Adapted from THE DOG WHO CAME TO DINNER by Sydney Taylor. Copyright © 1966, by Follett Publishing Company. Used by permission of Follett Publishing Company; and for "The O'Learys Make Friends." Adapted from THE O'LEARYS AND FRIENDS by Jean Horton Berg. Copyright © 1961, by Follett Publishing Company.

(Acknowledgments continue on page 256.)

Project Director: Ralph J. Cooke
Senior Editor: Helen W. Crane
Editor: Marilyn L. Maples
Production Director: LaVergne Niequist
Senior Production Editor: Sonja Sola
Production Editor: Angela Zabransky
Art Director: Gloria Muczynski
Art Consultants: Donald Meighan, Don Walkoe
Cover Art: Donald Charles
Illustrators: Angela Adams, Marc Belenchia, Ted Carr, Pat Doyle, June Goldsborough, Hilary Hayton, Dora Leder, Erica Merkling, Larry Mikec, Charles Mitchell, Krystyna Orska, Sylvie Selig, Justin Wager, Hans Zander
Photographer: Bill Rogers

ISBN 0-8445-3148-0

Copyright © 1980 by
Laidlaw Brothers, Publishers
A Division of Doubleday & Company, Inc.

PRINTED IN THE UNITED STATES OF AMERICA

23456789 10 11 12 13 14 15   876543210

Contents

Fun to Know

Guess Again

Almost True

Finding a Way

Fun to Know

The O'Learys
Make Friends

The O'Leary family was in the yard
of their new house.

The children were just standing around.
They had no one to play with.

8

"I want to make some friends here,"
Polly O'Leary said.

"Me, too," said Wally O'Leary.

"It's not hard to make friends,"
said their mother. "Just wait and see."

Mr. O'Leary was looking at the house.
"I like this house," he said.
"Look up on the roof. Something on the roof
looks like a cat."

Mrs. O'Leary looked up at the roof.
And so did the little O'Learys.

"Looks like a cat? It is a cat!"
cried Mrs. O'Leary. "It's our Susan."

"How did she get way up there?"
asked Wally.

"I don't know how she got up there,"
said Mr. O'Leary. "And I don't know
how she will get down."

Then Mr. O'Leary looked at Susan
way up on the roof. "Here, kitty, kitty,"
he called.

Susan looked down at Mr. O'Leary.
But she did not come down.

Mr. O'Leary called again,
"Here, kitty, kitty, kitty!"

A big yellow cat ran up to Mr. O'Leary.

"Go away," Mr. O'Leary said.
"You are not the cat I want."

Mr. O'Leary looked up at Susan again.
"Here, kitty, kitty, kitty!" he called.

"Wait! Let me get her down,"
Mrs. O'Leary said.

"Susan, you silly thing!"
she cried. "Get down from there
this minute!"

"Silly thing, am I?" called the lady
next door.

"Oh, no, I mean Susan is silly,"
said Mrs. O'Leary.

"I am Susan!" said the lady.

"Oh, my," said Mrs. O'Leary.
"Susan is our cat. We were calling her.
She is up there on the roof."

Susan-the-lady looked up at Susan-the-cat.

"Well," said Susan-the-lady.

"We must get her down."

"We are trying," said Mrs. O'Leary.

"Here, kitty! Come down here, you silly cat!"

"We must make her want to come down," said Susan-the-lady. "Get some milk."

"We don't have any," said Wally.

"Come with me," said Susan-the-lady.
"We will get some bowls of milk
and put them all around your house.
When your cat sees the milk, she'll come down
in a minute."

Is putting out milk a good way to get
the cat down? Why?
What would you do?

Try Again, Mr. O'Leary

"I could reach out that window and get Susan," said Mr. O'Leary.

"Wait for the milk," said Mrs. O'Leary. "Susan will come down in a minute when she sees the bowls of milk."

"I want to get her down now," said Mr. O'Leary.

He ran into the house.

In a minute Mr. O'Leary put his head
out of the window. "Is Susan still up there?"
he asked.

"Right over your head," said Mrs. O'Leary.

"I can't reach her from here,"
Mr. O'Leary said. "Maybe she will jump to me!"
Then he called, "Here, kitty, kitty, kitty!"

"Wait for the milk," Mrs. O'Leary said.

"I can't wait," Mr. O'Leary said.
"I have an idea."

Then he went away.

In a minute Mr. O'Leary was back
with Wally's little chair.

Mr. O'Leary held the chair
out of the window.

He held it up as high as he could.

"Come on, Susan!" he called.
"Jump!" But Susan did not jump.

"I have a better idea,"
said Mr. O'Leary.

"Wait for the milk,"
said Mrs. O'Leary.

But Mr. O'Leary went away again.

17

Mrs. O'Leary looked up
and saw a mop come out
of the window.
Then out came
Mr. O'Leary's head.

"Now I can reach her,"
said Mr. O'Leary.

"Where is that lady
with the milk?"
asked Mrs. O'Leary.

Mr. O'Leary held the mop
in front of Susan.
"Here, kitty!" he called.
"Jump, kitty!"

But Susan would not
get on the mop.

A big, red-faced man ran into the yard.
"Stop, you!" he cried. "I saw you try
to hit that cat with a chair.
And now you are hitting her with a mop!
Stop it, or I'll call a policeman!"
  "Oh, my!" said Mrs. O'Leary.
And she sat down right where she was.
  "Help!" cried Mr. O'Leary.
"I can't hold up this mop any longer."

What will happen now?

Listen, Mother!

Susan-the-lady and the O'Leary children ran into the yard. Other people ran after them.

"I didn't have enough milk at my house," said Susan-the-lady. "But I got some from the neighbors. And they have come to help us. What is happening now?"

In the window, Mr. O'Leary was trying to hold up the mop.

In the yard, the neighbors were running around putting milk into bowls.

Cats came running into the yard to drink the milk. More cats kept coming.

More and more neighbors kept coming. Everyone told the O'Learys what to do.

"Call a policeman!" said one neighbor.

"Get the firemen!" said another neighbor.

"Get a long ladder!" said the big, red-faced man.

"And stop trying to hit that cat!"

"Mother," said Polly O'Leary.
"Listen, Mother——"

"Wait, Polly," said Mrs. O'Leary.

"But, Mother——"

"Wait, Polly!" said Mrs. O'Leary.
"They are bringing a ladder.
Let's see what will happen!"

"But, Mother——!"

One of the neighbors put the ladder up
to the roof. He climbed up and looked.
"No cat here," he called.

"Mother!" Polly said in a loud voice.
"Listen, Mother——"

"Wait, Polly!" Mrs. O'Leary kept saying.

Then she called to the neighbor,
"There has to be a cat up there. Our Susan
is up there."

"I don't see any cat," said the neighbor.
And he began to climb down.

Then Polly O'Leary said
in a loud, LOUD voice,
"Mother, I've been trying to tell you!
Susan is back of the house
drinking milk!"
    "Oh, my!" Mrs. O'Leary cried
in a loud voice. "Susan climbed down
all by herself!"
    Mrs. O'Leary looked around.
She looked at all the neighbors.
"Wait a minute," called Mrs. O'Leary.
Then she went into the house.

25

Soon Mrs. O'Leary came out with an ice-cold
orange drink for everyone.

She looked around at all her neighbors.
"See," she said to Mr. O'Leary and the children.
"I told you it is not hard to make friends!"

Cat Bath

After she eats,
my purry friend
washes herself
from end to end,

Washes her face,
her ears, her paws,
washes the pink
between her claws.

I watch, and think
it's better by far
to splash in a tub
with soap in a bar

And washcloth in hand
and towel on the rung
than have to do all
that work *by tongue*.

Aileen Fisher

The Dog Who Came to Dinner

Mr. Stone looked at the empty house next door.

"That house has been empty for a long time," he said.

"There is still no name on the mailbox."

"And it is such a nice house, too,"
said Mrs. Stone. "I wish some nice family
would move into it."

"A family with a girl," said Jane.

"A family with a boy," said Jimmy.

The Stone family got into their car
and went to see Mr. Stone's mother.
They stayed at her house overnight.

When the family came home the next day,
Mr. Stone said, "Look! There is a name
on the mailbox in front of the empty house!"

Jimmy jumped out of the car and ran to look.
"The name on the mailbox is LANE," he said.

"Oh, how nice!" said Mrs. Stone.
"Someone moved into the house
while we were away."

"We must make them feel at home,"
said Mr. Stone.

"Yes," said his wife. "I will ask them
to come to our house for dinner tomorrow."

The next night Mr. Stone
opened the door.
In came Mr. and Mrs. Lane.
In came Peter and Peggy Lane.
And
in came
a big dog!

"How do you do?" said Mr. Stone.

"How do you do?" said Mr. Lane.

"It was nice of you to ask us to dinner,"
said Mrs. Lane.

"We are happy to have you," said Mrs. Stone.
"Please feel at home.
Dinner will be ready soon."

They all went
into the living room.
Mr. and Mrs. Stone talked
to Mr. and Mrs. Lane.
Jimmy and Jane Stone talked
to Peter and Peggy Lane.

The big dog began
to run around
and wag his tail.
He was ready to play.

The dog ran over to Mr. Stone
and began to bark.

Mr. Stone petted him. "Nice dog," he said.

The dog ran to Mrs. Stone
and sniffed her hand.
Then he put his front paws in her lap.

"Oh!" cried Mrs. Stone.

Now the dog ran to Jane. He sniffed her shoe.
Then he wagged his tail and put his paws
in her lap.

Peggy started to stand up. But the dog barked
and jumped up, trying to lick her face.
Peggy fell down on top of Jane.
Everyone laughed.

The dog seemed to be laughing, too.
He wanted to play. He ran round and round
the living room, trying to catch his tail.
Soon he ran to Peter and Jimmy. They petted him.

He chewed Peter's shoe and licked his hand.
Then he poked his nose into Jimmy's face
and jumped all over him.

"He likes to play," said Peter.

"Yes," Jimmy said. "See how his tail
is wagging. And how he licks my face."

Now the dog smelled something sweet.
He barked. Then he poked his nose
into the candy.

Crunch! He chewed some candy.

Crunch! Crunch!

He chewed some more candy.

The dog ran to another nice smell.

He was still wagging his tail.

He poked his nose into the cookies.

Crunch! He chewed a cookie.

Crunch! Crunch!

He chewed some more cookies.

The children laughed. "He likes sweets!"
they cried. "He likes candy and cookies."
Mr. and Mrs. Stone did not laugh.
They looked at Mr. and Mrs. Lane.
But they did not say anything.

Mr. and Mrs. Lane looked
at Mr. and Mrs. Stone.
But they did not say anything.

Why didn't Mr. and Mrs. Lane say anything?
What were Mr. and Mrs. Stone thinking?

Dinner Is Ready

Mrs. Stone said, "Dinner is ready."

Everyone went into the dining room and sat down.

The big dog took another cookie from the plate.

Then he went into the dining room, too. But he did not sit down.

The big dog ran round and round
the dining room. He put his front paws
on the table and smelled Mr. Lane's plate.
He poked his nose into Mrs. Lane's plate.
He licked Jane's plate. His front paws
went all over Jimmy's plate.
He wagged his tail.

Mr. and Mrs. Stone did not want
the dog's paws on their plates.
They looked at Mr. and Mrs. Lane.
But they did not say anything.

Mr. and Mrs. Lane did not tell the dog
to stop.

They looked at Mr. and Mrs. Stone.
But they, too, did not say anything.

Then Mr. Stone asked,
"What is the name of your dog?"

"Our dog?" said Mr. Lane.

"He is not our dog!"
cried Mrs. Lane.

"But he came in with you!"
said Jane.

"Oh!" said Mrs. Stone.

"This dog was standing in front
of your house," Peter said.

"So we thought he was your dog!" cried Peggy.

"Our dog?" said Mr. Stone.

"He is not our dog!" said Mrs. Stone.

"Oh!" said Mrs. Lane.

Then Mrs. Stone said, "He is not your dog,
and he is not our dog. Who does he belong to?"

"He must belong to someone!"
Jimmy cried. "He has a collar."

Mr. Stone looked at the collar.

"Who does he belong to?"
asked Peggy.

"He belongs to a family
on the next block,"
said Mr. Stone. "Their name is
on the collar."

"He lives on the next block!"
cried Jane. "Why did he come
to our house?"

"He wants to make friends, too,"
said Mrs. Lane.

"So he came to dinner,"
said Mrs. Stone.

Everyone laughed.
The dog barked
and wagged his tail.

"The dog poked his nose into all our plates," said Mrs. Stone.

"Come, Jane, we must wash them.
  Then we will have our dinner."

  "And the dog, too?" cried the children.

  "Yes," said Mr. Stone.
"The dog will have some dinner, too.
  Let's get a bone for him to chew."

When dinner was over, they all went into the living room and sat down.

"That was such a nice dinner," said Mrs. Lane.

"I am glad you liked it," said Mrs. Stone.

"Arf! Arf!" barked the dog.

"He liked the dinner, too," said Peggy.

"Yes," said Peter. "See how his tail is wagging."

The dog ran to the door. He put
his front paws on it. "Arf! Arf!" he barked.

Jimmy said, "Dinner is over. Now he wants
to go to his home."

Everyone laughed. The dog seemed
to be laughing, too. He barked again
and wagged his tail.

Mr. Stone opened the door.

The dog who came to dinner

ran

all the way

home.

Wishing

If I could have
Any wish that could be

I'd wish that a dog
Could have me.

Eve Merriam

45

A Pet in a Bowl

Ah Jim lived in Chinatown.

From the window of his apartment

he could look down on balconies and rooftops.

On the balconies of the houses
his neighbors watered their window-box gardens
and played with their pets.

On one of the balconies there was a woman
who had a big red and gold bird. And there was
a man with a black cat on the back of his chair.

Ah Jim liked to watch the bird and the cat.

47

One day Ah Jim had been watching the pets
on the balconies. He said to his mother,
"I would like to have a pet."

Ah Jim's mother was cooking dinner.
She didn't even look at him.

He said it three times
before his mother answered him.

"Our family is big and our apartment
is small," she said. "There is not much room.
But you may have a small pet. It must be
little enough to fit in a rice bowl."

Ah Jim watched his mother.
She just went on
with her cooking.

At dinner Ah Jim ate his rice.
When it was all gone, he looked
at his rice bowl. It was very small.
What kind of a pet would fit in it?

"I don't know what pet I want," he said.

Ah Jim's brothers laughed at him.

"Do you want a turtle?" they asked.
"Do you want a cricket?"

But Ah Jim didn't know.

After dinner his oldest brother said,
"Forget about your pet. Come with us to see
a play. You will like it."

There were red and yellow animals
in the play. Ah Jim liked the animals,
but they were only made of paper.
Paper animals were not much fun.

What Will Fit?

The next morning Ah Jim went to school.
He worked hard all morning.
Then he ate in the big school yard
with his friends.

"Do you have a pet?" he asked Tony.

"I have a little turtle in a glass bowl,"
said his friend.

"I have a cricket in a cage,"
said Ping Loo.

A turtle or a cricket would be small enough
to fit in a rice bowl. But Ah Jim
would have to keep the turtle in a glass bowl
and the cricket in a small cage.

The turtle would not be free to swim.
And the cricket would not be free to jump.

Ah Jim knew that he didn't want a cricket
in a cage. Or a turtle in a glass bowl.

"What kind of a pet do I want?" he thought.
"Do I want a firefly? Do I want a goldfish?"

"No," thought Ah Jim. "A firefly
would not be free to fly. And a goldfish
could only swim around in its glass house."

The next day Ah Jim looked
at his rice bowl again.

"I'll take it with me," he said.
"And I'll find a pet that will fit."

He walked up the hill to the Chinatown shops.
Every shop had things to look at.
In the large window of one shop
he saw a very small green elephant.

"There is something that would go
in my rice bowl," he said.

But Ah Jim did not want the green elephant.
He wanted a live pet.

Through the large window, he saw something
run across the shop. It was a little dog,
the littlest he had ever seen.
It was the color of gold. It had two black eyes
and a little, round nose.
It jumped into a small basket.

The dog would make a nice pet.
It was just about what he wanted, but not quite.
It would not fit in the rice bowl.

Ah Jim looked through the shop window again.
The glass was cold against his nose.
Two black eyes looked back at him
from over the side of the basket.

Try the Pet Shop

The man who owned the shop came outside.
"Don't put your hands and face
against my window," he said. "Boys and girls
come to look at the dog in my shop. And I must
always wash this window after they leave."

Ah Jim hurried away, carrying his empty bowl.
He was hungry, so he ran right home for lunch.

After his lunch, Ah Jim went out to play.
He still carried his rice bowl.

At the top of the hill his brothers
were flying their kites. The kites
looked like large golden birds.
Ah Jim stopped to watch them.

He thought about the golden dog he had seen
in the store. If only it were small enough
to fit in his rice bowl! But it wasn't. Not quite.

"Look at our hungry brother,"
said the oldest brother. "He is carrying
his rice bowl in his hand."

"He doesn't know what he wants to put in it,"
said the second brother.

"Why don't you go to the pet shop?"
asked the third brother. "You might see
something little there."

Ah Jim watched the kites up in the sky.
After a few minutes he walked away
toward the pet shop. On his way
Ah Jim met a boy from his school.

"What are you carrying?" asked Ah Jim.

"A frog," the boy said.

"Can I hold it?" Ah Jim asked.

The boy held Ah Jim's bowl, and Ah Jim
held the frog. One minute the frog
was in his hands, and the next minute
it was gone.

The frog had hopped
inside Ah Jim's shirt.

Ah Jim hopped, too. He reached
inside his shirt for the frog.

"I don't want a frog," he thought.
"It is too cold. I want a warm pet."

At the pet shop, Ah Jim saw
quite a few animals. He saw a monkey,
a red and green bird, and a black cat.
But they were all too big for his rice bowl.

He wanted a pet he could hold. He wanted
a pet that was warm, a pet that would fit
in his rice bowl.

Ah Jim could not forget the golden dog,
the dog that was almost little enough
to fit in his rice bowl.

Ah Jim turned back toward Chinatown.
In a few minutes he reached the shop
where he had seen the green elephant.

He put his face against the window.
The little dog was still there. Ah Jim
wanted that dog. He didn't want the monkey.
And he didn't want the frog that had jumped
inside his shirt.

The man who owned the shop came outside.

"You again!" he said. "You come
to look through my window. So I wash off
finger marks and face marks all day long.
Please go."

Ah Jim saw that the window was almost covered
with marks. He turned and ran.

Around the corner he stopped. He thought
about all the finger marks on the window,
the marks he had made. He turned
and went back to the shop.

Another Small Golden Dog

The shopkeeper was starting to wash the window.
It was almost covered with marks
left by fingers and faces.

Ah Jim said to the shopkeeper,
"I would like to wash the window for you."

"But the marks are not all your finger marks,"
said the shopkeeper.

"I know," said Ah Jim. "But many of them are.
I will wash the window."

"Very good," said the shopkeeper.

Ah Jim set his rice bowl down on the walk
and started to work. He began to clean and shine
the window. While he worked, he watched
the golden dog. Soon the window
was clean and bright.

Ah Jim looked inside the shop. He saw
the shopkeeper and his wife laughing.

"Come in, come in," the shopkeeper called.
"My wife and I have thought of a very good thing."

Ah Jim went inside.

"Tomorrow the mother dog goes back to China
with our brother," the shopkeeper said.
"Our brother will leave one puppy here."
He reached inside a small basket.

There in the shopkeeper's hand
was the smallest puppy Ah Jim had ever seen.
The man handed it to him carefully.

"Now," said the shopkeeper. "Take this puppy.
Then the children will not come to our window.
They will not put their noses and hands
against our clean glass. I will not have
to shine it, for the dogs will be gone."

The puppy was the color of gold.
It was warm. And it was just right
to fit into the rice bowl.

Ah Jim was so happy he could not speak.
He tried to thank the shopkeeper and his wife.
But no words came.

The woman smiled. "Do not speak," she said.
"We see your thanks in your face."

Ah Jim walked down the street,
carefully carrying the puppy in his rice bowl.
He did not stop to speak to anyone.
He walked down the hill and into his apartment.
"LOOK," he cried. "It fits in my rice bowl!"
His brothers laughed, and after a while,
his mother laughed, too.
And Ah Jim laughed the longest of all.

A Delicious Day

All week Miss Youngbird's class
had been reading about the kinds of work
that people do.

Miss Youngbird had said, "Over the weekend
think about the work that someone
in your family does. Next week
you can tell us a true story about it."

Monday came, and Linda was ready to tell
her true story.

She held up a bag and said,

"Hold out your hand
And close your eyes.
I'll give you something
To make you wise."

67

All the boys and girls closed their eyes.
As Linda walked around the circle,
she put something into everyone's hand.

Why, it was candy! Chocolate candy!

As the children sat in the circle,
they began to wonder. Why was Linda
giving them candy?

"My grandmother made that candy
in a factory," Linda said.

"In a factory?" asked Jim.

All the children liked the chocolate candy.
And they all wanted some more.

"I wonder how your grandmother makes
this candy," said Carol.

"Where does she live?" asked Ken.

"Just a minute," said Linda.
"If you'll give me time, I'll tell you
all about my grandmother's job
and the candy she makes."

Then Linda began to tell her true story.

Linda's Story

Last summer Mom and I went to visit
my grandmother. I knew she had a new job.
But I didn't know what kind of work she did.

When we got to Grandmother's house,
she wasn't home. My mom let us in the house,
and we went into the living room.

The house was very quiet.
All you could hear was the ticktock of a clock.

Three goldfish were swimming slowly
in their large, glass bowl.

A big, black cat was sleeping
in a chair by the window.
But there was no sign
of Grandmother.

"I wonder where Grandmother is?" I asked.

"Maybe she is at work," answered Mom.

I went into the kitchen. There was a paper on the kitchen table.

It said,

Hi!
Come to the big factory
on River Street.
Come in the front door.
Ask for me.

Love,
Nan

Nan is my grandmother, and she was still at work.

"Would you like to visit Grandmother
at work?" asked Mom.

"Hey," I said. "It would be fun to see
what Grandmother's job is."

We walked to the factory on River Street.
The factory was very large.
It was two city blocks long!

As we got near the factory, Mom and I
smelled something wonderful. It smelled sweet.
It smelled good. It smelled like chocolate.

"That's a good sign," said Mom.
"They must be making chocolate candy today."

We went in the front door.

A man who was sitting there asked,

"May I help you?"

Mom told him who we wanted
to see. The man told us to wait.
Then he walked off.

In a few minutes he came back.
Grandmother was with him.
She had a big smile on her face.
And I could tell she was happy
to see us.

"Hi!" she said. "I'm glad
you got here. Would you like
to see the factory?"

"Would I!" I answered. "Can we watch
the people making candy?"

"You sure can," laughed Grandmother.
"Come on. I'll show you."

"What do you do here?" I asked.

"Just wait. You'll see,"
she answered.

Grandmother Makes Candy

We started to walk through the factory.
We smelled wonderful, sweet smells
that were coming from a very large kitchen.

"Can we go in there?" I asked.

"No, but we can watch from the doorway,"
said Grandmother.

"Wow, look at those pots!" I said.

"We cook the chocolate in those pots,"
my grandmother said.

Men and women were busy everywhere.
They were all wearing clean, white clothes.

"What a busy place!" Mom said.
"And see how clean the kitchen is."

"Yes," said Grandmother. "We must keep
everything very clean. That is why everyone
is wearing white clothes."

We listened to the noise the machines made
as the hot chocolate was lifted into the air.

Across the room some women were working
with a machine that put the chocolate
into a large pan. The chocolate was running
into little squares in the pan.

"What are those women doing?" I asked.

"They are putting the candy into a mold,"
Grandmother answered.

"A mold? What is a mold?" I asked.

"Do you see that woman over there
lifting that large pan?" asked Grandmother.

"Yes," I answered.

"Well, that pan is called a mold,"
Grandmother told me.

"Some candy is round and some candy is square," said Grandmother.
"To make square candy, the women use a mold that has many little squares in it.
A machine puts chocolate into each square.
Then the chocolate is left to cool.
Next, it is taken out of the mold.
The candy will be square, like the mold."

"You mean they make square candy in a mold like that?" I asked.
"Do they make round candy the same way?"

"They sure do," answered Grandmother.
"And that is my job. I run a machine that puts the chocolate into a round mold."

"That looks like fun," I said.

Grandmother laughed. "Come on," she said.
"Let's go to the next room."

We went with her and watched
from a doorway again. In this room
a machine was putting paper around some candy.
Another machine was putting the candy into boxes.

Just about this time I got a funny feeling.

"I feel funny inside," I said. "I wonder why."

"I think I know," said my mom.
"You're hungry. We didn't have any lunch.
Besides, this place would make anyone hungry."

"I can fix that," said Grandmother.
"I'll get you some of the candy I just made."

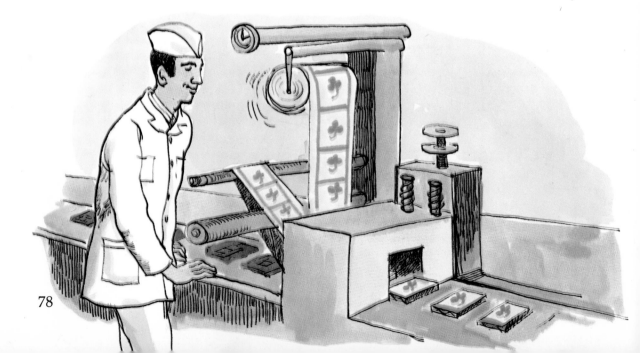

As I ate the candy, I said,

"Now let me see if I can remember everything.

First of all, the candy has to cook.

Then it is put into a mold to cool.

Next, some paper is put around it.

Last of all, a machine puts the candy

into boxes. Then it is sent

all over the country."

"Wow!" I said to Grandmother.

"What a great job! Just think.

You get to work a chocolate machine.

You get to make candy all day long!"

Linda sat down.

"That was a great story," said Ken.

"I wish I had a grandmother with a job like that.
I'd eat candy all day."

Miss Youngbird walked over to Linda.

She smiled as she said,

"Linda, you told us something
To make us wise.
Now close your eyes
For your surprise."

How could Miss Youngbird surprise Linda?

How to Make Chocolate Candy

Would you like to make some chocolate candy?
This is what you must do.

1. Put a 12 oz. bag of semisweet chocolate bits into a pan.

2. Heat the chocolate until it is soft.

3. Then add:
   2/3 cup sweetened condensed milk
   1 tablespoon of water
   1 teaspoon of vanilla

4. Spread the mix evenly in a flat pan.

5. When the chocolate is hard, cut into squares with a knife.

Happy eating!

A Job in the Sky

The next morning it was Ken's turn
to tell his story. He held up a pair
of tiny silver wings.

"My dad wears silver wings like these,"
he said. "Can you guess what his job is?"

"I wonder," said Carol.
"Does your father work
at the airport?"

"You're almost right,"
said Ken. "But not quite."

Then Ken began to tell
about his father's job.

Ken's Story

My dad is an airplane pilot.
He flies large airplanes all over the world.
He takes people from this country to airports
in other countries of the world.

Quite often Dad brings back many things
for people to buy in stores.
And once in a while, he brings animals
from zoos in other lands
to the zoos in this country.

My dad isn't home very much.
Just like other pilots, he is often gone
for many days at a time.

I never know what he'll bring home.
It could be almost anything
that can be carried in an airplane.

One time he brought a boat
for our neighbor.
It was almost too big to fit
into an airplane.

Another time he brought
two clocks. One clock was so big
I could almost stand in it.

Once he even brought
six wooden shoes.
But the shoes weren't empty.
They had two boys and a girl
in them.

The children were going
to visit their father
at the United Nations Building.

Before my mom's last birthday, I wanted
Dad to bring back a present to surprise her.
I thought and thought about it.
What would be a nice present for Mom?

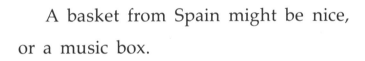

    A basket from Spain might be nice,
or a music box.
    The day before Dad went away,
I told him about my idea.
    "I'll do my best," he said. "But until
I get a telephone call from the airport,
I won't know where I'll be going next.
I'll try to see what I can do.
Maybe I can bring back a birthday present
to surprise Mom."

Five days went by.

I thought I couldn't wait

to see what Dad would bring home.

We had a telephone call from him

when he was at an airport in Spain.

Then he made a quick call from Canada

to tell us that he was already on his way home.

When I talked to him on the telephone,

I asked, "Did you get a music box or a basket

when you were in Spain?"

"No," he answered.

"Did you get something else for Mom?" I asked.

"Well, yes and no," he answered.

"It's a secret. When I come home tomorrow,

you'll see what I mean."

"Oh, boy!" I thought. "Dad didn't get

a music box or a basket. What else could he

have found? What did Dad mean by 'yes and no'?

And what could the secret be?"

A Birthday Surprise

Dad came home the next day.
I saw his car drive up.
What kind of a present would he have?

I watched him get out of the car.
He wasn't carrying anything
that looked like a present.

"Boy! Oh, boy!" I thought.
"Mom's birthday is already here.
Why doesn't Dad have her present
with him?"

As Dad came into the house,
he called, "Quick, Ken.
Get a bowl of water
and take it out to the car."

"What for?" I asked.
"Why do you need water?"

"Take the water out
and you'll see," said Dad.

I quickly ran out to the car with the water.
Dad came right behind me.

And there on the back seat of the car
was a seal in a cage!

"Wow!" I said. "Is that the secret?
Is that for Mom's birthday?"

"What do you think?" asked Dad.
"Mom has always wanted a fur coat.
Now here is one.
But the owner is still wearing it."

Just then Mom came
out of the house.

"What in the world
is in our car?" she asked.

"Look, Mom," I called.
"Here is the fur coat
you've always wanted.
It's your birthday present.
But the seal goes with it."

Mom laughed and said,
"I know I've always wanted a fur coat.
But that coat doesn't belong on me.
It belongs on the seal,
and he should keep on wearing it.
I'm sure he needs a fur coat
more than I do."

Dad reached inside the car.

"I'm glad you liked my secret,"
he said to me.

Then he handed Mom a box.

"Here's your real birthday present,"
he told her. "It flew all the way from Spain
in my airplane."

I wondered what could be inside that box.
I knew it couldn't be a basket or a music box.

What could be in the box Dad brought?

Ken sat down.

"Do you mean the seal really flew
to this country in an airplane?" Jim asked.

"He sure did!" answered Ken.

"Did you get to keep the seal?" asked Carol.

"No," said Ken. "Dad just thought
it would be fun for us to see the seal
before he took it to the zoo."

Then Ken opened a box.
Inside were more tiny silver wings.

"Here's a pair of silver wings
for everyone," he said.
"Dad brought them from the airport.
He thought you'd like to have
your own wings. Who knows?
Someday maybe one of you
will be a pilot, too."

A Left-handed Surprise

The next morning Miss Youngbird looked at Jim and said, "Would you like to tell us a story today?"

"I sure would," said Jim. "But I can't tell about my dad's job. Because I don't have a dad living at home. I'd like to tell about my uncle and the baseball game."

All the boys and girls wanted to hear Jim's story. So he began to tell it.

Jim's Story

A few weeks ago, when I came home from school, I looked for Mom. I found her in the kitchen cooking dinner.

"Mmmm! What smells so good?" I asked.

"I'm making bean soup with carrots," answered Mom.

I sat down at the kitchen table and looked out the window.

"You don't look very happy," said Mom. "Did something happen at school today?"

"No," I said. "But I've been wondering.
Why do I have to be left-handed?
All my friends are right-handed."

"I don't think anyone really knows
the answer to that," Mom said.

I watched her as she cut up meat and carrots
to put into the pot of bean soup.

"See," I said. "You are right-handed, too."

"Well," said Mom. "All people are not alike.
We are all different in one way or another."

"But I don't like
to be different," I said.
"You wouldn't like it, either.
When I write, I have to turn
my paper around.
And I think it looks funny."
"Is that all?" asked Mom.
"No," I answered.
"Quite often when I eat,
my arm hits the boy sitting
next to me."
"That doesn't seem
too important," said Mom.
"Maybe not to you," I said.
"But I'll tell you
what really is important.
When I play baseball,
and it's my turn to catch,
I can't find a mitt to fit me.
Every mitt we have
is for a right-handed player."

Mom looked up at me and smiled.

"Well, Jim," she said.
"Lots of people are left-handed.
Most of them don't seem to mind
being a little bit different.
The day might come
when you won't mind, either.
Try not to let being left-handed
bother you."

But it did bother me.
I wanted to be right-handed
like everyone else.
Well, almost everyone else.

How could I ever be a great baseball player
if I couldn't even find a mitt to fit me?

Do you ever think that you are different
from other children? In what way?

Later in the week I got
a telephone call. It was Uncle Jack.
His baseball team, the Mets,
was coming to town for a game.

"Would you like to go to the game?"
asked Uncle Jack. "I can get seats
for you and your mom."

"Well, I guess so," I answered.

"What's wrong?" asked Uncle Jack.
"You don't seem very excited
about going to the game."

"Oh, nothing is really wrong,"
I told him. "I do want to see
a baseball game more than anything else.
And I just know the game
will be lots of fun. We'll be there!"

"OK, Jim. See you and your mother
at the game next week,"
said Uncle Jack.

Uncle Jack's Two Surprises

When the big day came, Mom and I went
to the baseball field. We got there
long before game time.

Uncle Jack had picked some good seats
for us right near the wall.
From there we could watch both teams.

The Mets were out in the field,
but I couldn't see Uncle Jack.
Two players were taking turns hitting balls
to the men in the outfield.
Other players were throwing balls
to each other.

After a few minutes Mom said,
"That player just hit a fly to left field.
Watch the left fielder throw it back."

"Hey, he throws with his left hand!" I shouted.

Then I began to look around the field at the other players.

"Look!" I called. "The first baseman is throwing left-handed!"

I looked again. Not only was he using his left hand, but that hand belonged to someone I knew. And that someone was Uncle Jack!

"Wow!" I shouted in an excited voice. "Even Uncle Jack throws left-handed!"

Just then I saw Uncle Jack
begin to run toward us.

"Hi!" he called. He reached over the wall
and handed me something. "You can have
lots of fun with this, Jim. It's my old mitt.
I'm going to begin using a new one this week."

What a great surprise! Was I ever excited!

"Who knows," I thought. "Someday I might
be out there on the other side of the wall.
I might be throwing and hitting the ball
left-handed. Just like Uncle Jack. I might
even be playing for the Mets team."

Yes, it was a great day—an exciting,
wonderful day. Only one thing was wrong.
The Mets lost the game, and I was sorry.

Jim sat down.

"Show us your baseball," said Ken.

"Oh, yes, I almost forgot," Jim said.
He reached into his pocket and pulled out
a baseball. It was covered with writing.

He held up the ball and said,
"On this ball are the names
of all the players on my uncle's team."

"Just think," said Ken.
"I wonder what it would be like
to play baseball every day."

"And to have someone pay you
for playing a game,"
laughed Carol.

Four Clues

The next morning Ken said,
"I'm really sorry that storytime
is over. I sure wish someone else
had a true story to tell."

Jim looked at Miss Youngbird.
"How about you?" he asked.

"Well," said Miss Youngbird.
"My mother has a job.
Would you like to hear about it?"

"Of course!" said Carol.
"Each of us had a turn.
Now it's your turn."

Miss Youngbird's Game

Miss Youngbird smiled. "I have another idea," she said. "Instead of just listening to a story, how would you like to play a game?"

This was different! The boys and girls began to wonder what kind of a game they would play.

Miss Youngbird said, "All of you know that my mother is an American Indian. Suppose I give you some clues about her job. Listen for each clue. Then see if you are able to guess what kind of job she has."

"Oh, I know how to play this game,"
said Carol. "If we want to win,
we have to guess your mother's job."

"That's right," Miss Youngbird said.
"If I give you just a few clues,
do you suppose you'll be able to guess?"

The children thought that a guessing game
would be fun. Of course, each of them wanted
to win. So they tried to remember everything
they had heard about American Indians.

Miss Youngbird started the game
by giving a clue.

She said, "To do her work on time,
my mother has to get up early each morning."

"I'll bet she gets up early
to hunt food for breakfast," said Kay.

Miss Youngbird laughed. "No, Kay," she said.
"My mother doesn't hunt food for breakfast.
Instead, she buys food at a store,
just as other people do."

"Let's go on with the game!"
shouted the boys and girls.
"Give another clue to help us guess."

"Some children might have tired feet
if my mother didn't do her job,"
said Miss Youngbird.

"Tired feet?" asked Carol.

"Oh, I bet I know!" shouted Ken.
"She makes soft shoes
from the hides of animals."

Miss Youngbird smiled.
"That's a good guess," she said.
"But most Indian women
don't make shoes
as they did long ago."

Then she asked, "Does anyone else have
a different idea about my mother's job?"

Not one of the children had an idea.

"OK," said Miss Youngbird.
"Then you will have to keep guessing.
I'll try to help you.
Here's the next clue."

Miss Youngbird said, "My mother
does something for boys and girls.
But sometimes they jump and shout.
Once in a while she has to tell them
to sit down and be quiet."

"Is she the one who builds a fire
when the Indians set up camp?" asked Jim.

"Does she tell the boys and girls to sit
around the fire and listen while she tells
stories?" asked Ted.

"No," answered Miss Youngbird. "Your guesses
are quite good. But all of you are thinking
about the way Indians lived in camps many years
ago. Indians don't often build campfires
these days. Besides, my mother is too busy.
And she does all her cooking in the kitchen.
Just as your mothers do."

Miss Youngbird smiled at the boys and girls. She said, "You still haven't guessed what my mother's job is. Do you give up?"

Everyone thought very hard. Miss Youngbird's mother didn't hunt food for her breakfast. She didn't make shoes or build campfires. What could her job be?

The boys and girls really wanted to win the game. They wanted another chance.

"Give us one more clue!" they shouted.

"OK," said Miss Youngbird. "This will be your last chance to guess. Without my mother's help, many children would not be able to go to school each day."

School? Everyone wondered how Miss Youngbird's mother could help children go to school.

Ted said, "Let's give up. I'm tired of guessing."

"Me, too," said Linda. "Tell us what your mother's job is."

"You gave us four different clues and we still can't guess," said Ken.

"She drives a school bus," said Miss Youngbird.

"A school bus!" said Ted. "No wonder she gets up so early in the morning."

Then Miss Youngbird said, "Indian women have many kinds of jobs these days. Some of them work in large stores and small shops. Some run machines in factories. Others have jobs in schools or in places where people eat."

Miss Youngbird showed the children
a picture. She said, "Here is my mother
and the bus she drives."

"Do you suppose you could ask her
to come and visit our class sometime?"
asked Ken.

"I could," answered Miss Youngbird.
"But don't look for her to drive up
in a school bus. If she comes, I'm sure
she will be driving her own car."

A Lazy Thought

There go the grownups
To the office,
To the store.
Subway rush,
Traffic crush;
Hurry, scurry,
Worry, flurry.

No wonder
Grownups
Don't grow up
Any more.

It takes a lot
Of slow
To grow.

Eve Merriam

Almost True

The Farmer and the Troll

There was once a man who owned a small farm.
All through the year he worked hard taking care
of his farm.

In the spring the farmer would dig
up the ground, to get ready to plant his crops.

In the summer and fall he would drive
into town. The wagon was always carrying food
from the farm—milk, eggs, apples,
or other things to eat.

One day everything started to go wrong.
The fresh milk began to sour. The eggs broke
when the farmer's wife picked them up.

The neighbor's dog started
to dig for bones in the garden.

Birds ate the plants
before they were ready
to be used.

And the crows poked holes
in the ears of corn
before the crop was ready
to be picked.

115

"What in the world is going on?"
asked the farmer's wife.
"Why does our fresh milk turn sour?
Why do we have broken eggs? Why are
the crows poking holes in our corn?
And what about the other strange things
that are happening?"

"I bet I know," said the farmer. "A troll
is behind this! Come on out to the milk house
with me. I'll show you what I have found."

There on the white floor
of the milk house
were many strange marks.
These same marks
were all over the path
to the garden.

"Of course it's a troll,"
said the farmer's wife.
"Those marks must mean
that a troll has come
to live on our farm."

That night she watched from a window.
Sure enough! There in the garden was a light—
a strange light hopping around on the path.
In those days everyone knew that a strange light
might be the shining eye of a troll.

So that was why these things were happening!
A troll had come to live on the farm.

The next morning the wife said to the farmer,
"Last night I saw a strange, bright light
on the garden path. It must have been a troll!"

The farmer was surprised. When a troll
came to live on a farm, most people felt
it was a sign of good luck.

But this troll was different.
He brought trouble with him.

Most trolls didn't need much
to keep them happy.

Sometimes a troll liked to have
a glass of milk or a pot of soup
set out for him on the kitchen steps.

And once in a while, on a cold, dark night,
a troll might come secretly into the living room
to warm himself by the fire. His one eye
would shine in the dark like a circle of light.

"Maybe this troll is cross
because I haven't put out any milk for him,"
said the farmer's wife. "I'll start
putting milk out on the steps tonight."

The farmer's wife put out
some milk every night.
And sometimes she put out
a pot of soup.

But that didn't help.
This cross troll just kept on
making trouble.

One night the farmer
said to his wife,
"I have thought and thought.
There just doesn't seem
to be an answer. My family
has lived on this farm
for hundreds of years.
They never had any trouble. But this morning
all the eggs broke. The fresh milk turned sour.
The neighbor's dog was digging in the garden.
And more birds got into our cornfield."

The farmer's wife felt that all the trouble
must be a sign of a bad-luck troll.

A Tricky Plan

One warm day in the spring the farmer
was digging in the field. He was getting ready
to plant potatoes.

All at once his horse stepped into a hole.
At the same time the farmer heard
a cross little voice. It seemed to be coming
from below the ground.

The voice said, "There you go again!
Poking through my roof. Don't you know
that I live below this hill?"

The farmer hardly knew what to think.
Could this be the troll talking?
And did the troll really think
the hill belonged to him?

The farmer thought to himself,
"That hill has belonged to my family
for over two hundred years. And this spring
I need to have the field to plant my potatoes.
What in the world am I going to do
about the troll?"

Just then the farmer had an idea.
He looked at the hole
where his horse had stepped.
Then he called down to the troll,
"Well now, Troll, I'm sorry
I had to dig in your hill.
But I have thought
of a very good plan."

"Ha! I bet," said the troll
in a cross voice.
"Well, don't just stand there.
Tell me your wonderful idea.
And don't try to trick me!"
"Each year I will plant and grow
something on this hill,"
said the farmer. "I will do
all the work myself.
At the end of the year
I will give you half of the crop
growing on your hill.
One year you can have the half
that grows above the ground,
and I will take the half
that grows below the ground."

The farmer looked around and said, "The next year you can have the half below the ground. And I will take the half above the ground. Doesn't that seem like a good idea?"

The troll thought for a few seconds. The plan seemed very good. It seemed almost too good to be true. He wondered if the farmer was trying to play a trick on him.

At last the troll said,
"Very well, your plan will do.
But this year I want the half
that grows above the ground."

The farmer covered his mouth with his hand.
He wanted to hide a smile. He was pleased.
You might even say he was very pleased.

Then he went on digging in the field.
He wanted to finish getting ready to plant
his potatoes.

As he planted them, he felt happy.
He was sure his trouble with this troll
was over.

When it was time to dig up the potatoes,
the troll climbed up through a hole in the hill.
He carefully broke off the tops
of almost one hundred potato plants
and took them down into the hole with him.
Later, he went back to finish the job.

"I like this plan," the troll thought
to himself. "Let the farmer have the roots
of the potatoes. I will take the part
above the ground."

When the next year came,
it was the troll's turn
to have all that grew
below the ground.

That spring, the farmer
had planted corn on the hill
over the troll's home.

That fall, when the corn crop
was high and golden yellow,
the troll was not seen
out in the farmer's field.
He was busy under the ground.
He was using his knife
to cut off the roots of the corn,
and he was feeling very happy
about the farmer's plan.

So year after year went by. One year
the farmer planted carrots. The troll
used his knife to cut off hundreds
of carrot tops. He let the farmer have the roots.

Another year, the farmer grew beans,
and he let the troll dig under the ground
for the bean roots.

Every year the troll got some of the crop.
And because he didn't have to work,
he thought he had played quite a trick
on the farmer.

But the farmer knew
who had played
the real trick.

What was the real trick?

Sing, Sack, Sing

In a small village there once lived
a mother with her only child, Rosita.
Because they did not have much money,
the mother had to work all day in the fields.

The fields were far away, so she
would leave home early in the morning
and not come back until late afternoon.

This left Rosita by herself all day,
and she was able to do very much as she wished.

One day as she sat by the door
of her house, she remembered what her mother
had told her about the river that ran
through the village.

"Never go near the river, my child,"
she had said. "For people say there was a time
when some children were carried away
and never brought back."

In the early afternoon,
after Rosita had finished her work
in the house, she closed the door
and went out for a walk.

As she walked slowly
down the road, she could feel
the hot sun on her back.

Rosita crossed field after field,
and soon found herself standing on the bank
of the very river her mother had talked about.

Looking down from the bank,
she could see tiny, silver fish
swimming about in the clear water.

Suddenly Rosita wanted to swim
in the cool water. By a nearby rock
she took off her dress. The last thing
she did was to take off her silver earrings
and put them on the rock.

Then she jumped into the river.
What a good time she had swimming
in the clear, cool water.

How long she was there, she could not tell.
But it was late afternoon when she started
to dress. The sun was going down as she hurried
toward home. She knew she must be there
before her mother came back from the fields.

Suddenly Rosita remembered her earrings.
She had left them on the rock near the river!

"What shall I do?" she said. "It will soon
be dark. Oh, my beautiful earrings!"

There was only one thing to do.
Rosita hurried back to the river.
She reached the place
where she had left the earrings.
There on the bank of the river
was a strange-looking man.
He had Rosita's earrings
in his hand.

"My earrings!" cried Rosita.
"I left them here while I was swimming.
Will you give them to me? I must get home
before my mother comes back from the fields."

"Here," said the man, holding out his hand.

As Rosita reached for her earrings,
the man took her by the arm.

"Let me go!" she cried.

But the man put her into a sack
and began to tie it shut.

Then he said, "You must stay in this sack.
When I tell you to sing, you must sing.
If you do not sing, I will beat the sack
with my stick."

Rosita was scared. She did not like to be
inside the sack. She wanted to be free.
She tried to climb out, but the sack was tied.

She thought to herself, "I must sing.
If I don't, the man will beat me with a stick.
The song could be important. It could help
to free me from this sack."

The man started toward a village
with the sack on his back.
All during the long walk,
Rosita thought how important
her song could be.
Then she had a clever idea.

A Clever Plan

During the next few days, the man went
from village to village with his sack.
At each village he would call out,
"Come here, people of this town,
and listen to my magic sack.
Listen to it sing."

Men, women, and children came running to stand around him. Then he would say in a loud voice:

"Sing, sack, sing.

Sing, and be quick.

Or I'll beat you with my stick."

Softly from the sack came a sweet voice:

"For my silver earrings

I was caught.

An important lesson

I've been taught."

People were pleased to hear the sweet voice that came from the sack. "How beautiful!" they called. "Do make it sing again." Every time the sack would sing, the man would get money from the people who were standing around.

From town to town went the man
with his sack. Everywhere he went,
the people went, too.

Then one day he came to the same town
where the little girl's mother lived.

He stopped at the village inn,
where people were eating their supper.
Later, when everyone had finished,
they wanted to hear his magic sack sing.

He took it and said:

"Sing, sack, sing.
Sing, and be quick.
Or I'll beat you with my stick."

Softly again came the sweet voice:

"For my silver earrings
I was caught.
An important lesson
I've been taught."

136

Now one of Rosita's friends happened to be among those who were listening. The song, coming from the sack, made her think of Rosita.

Could a little girl be inside the sack? Could the magic voice belong to Rosita?

Rosita's friend said the words of the song to herself. How clever! Yes, it had to be Rosita's voice. Rosita must be inside the sack.

Long after supper was over,
Rosita's friend went to the inn
to find the man. He was fast asleep,
so she could untie the sack.
And there was Rosita!

Very quickly the two girls left the room.
But they soon came back, carrying a basket
of mud and rocks to put in the empty sack.

In the morning the man picked up the sack and left the inn. At the first village where he stopped, he called the people to listen to his magic sack.

He said:

"Sing, sack, sing.
Sing, and be quick.
Or I'll beat you with my stick."

But no voice came out of the sack.

The people shouted, "Let us hear your magic sack!"

Again the man said:

"Sing, sack, sing.
Sing, and be quick.
Or I'll beat you with my stick."

Still no voice came from the sack.

Now the man was angry.

He beat on the sack with his stick.

At last it broke and rocks and mud
flew everywhere.

People were covered with mud.

They were so angry
they ran the man out of town,
and he was never seen again.

And you may be sure that Rosita never again
went to swim in the river which runs
through the village.

This is little Timothy Snail,
His house is on his back.

One day two men came along,

And popped him in a sack.
At last he managed to get out,
Out of a hole so small.

What became of him after that
I've never been told at all.

Author Unknown

What a Good Man Does Is Always Right

In an old farmhouse out in the country
there once lived a man and his wife.
The neighbors knew them as Mr. and Mrs. McMath.

They had never been rich, and their wants
were few. They owned only one thing
that anyone else might want—a horse.

One day the good wife looked up
from the bean soup she was making.
"We need other things more than that horse,"
she said. "Why not take him into town
and see what you can get for him?
Sell him or trade him for something useful.
Do what you think is best."

So off he went to sell the horse.
Mr. McMath was in the lead, and the horse
was walking along behind him. They had not
gone far when they met a farmer
leading a cow.

143

"Hello there!" called Mr. McMath.
"Who owns that cow?"

"Why, she belongs to me," was the answer.

"That's a fine cow," said Mr. McMath.
"I could use a cow as nice as that one.
Of course, a cow is not as good as a horse.
But I would like all the fresh, rich milk
she would give my wife and me.
Will you trade?"

The farmer thought he would like
to own a horse instead of a cow.
So the trade was made.

Mr. McMath might have gone home then.
But he had made up his mind to go into town.
So on he went, followed by the cow
that now belonged to him.

They walked quite fast and soon caught up
with a man who was leading a sheep.

"Now that is just what I need, my friend,"
said Mr. McMath to the owner of the sheep.
"A cow is useful, but it is also large.
On the other hand, a sheep is small—
small enough to take into the house
in the winter time. Would you like to trade?"

The man with the sheep was willing
to trade. So off he went with the cow
that gave fresh, rich milk.

Mr. McMath headed toward town,
followed this time by the sheep. But he soon
grew tired and stopped to rest beside a bridge.

He had not rested long when a man
with a large, white goose under his arm
came walking over the bridge.

"Sit down and rest a few minutes, my friend," said Mr. McMath. "What a heavy bird you have! It is fat and has lots of fine feathers. That goose would look just right standing in my backyard. Besides that, a goose can be useful. My wife could feed it carrot tops and other kitchen leftovers. As it is, she never knows what to do with them. How about it? Shall we trade? My sheep for your goose?"

The owner of the goose liked the idea of a trade. Besides, he was tired of carrying the heavy goose. So they traded, and Mr. McMath went on his way with the goose under his arm.

Wise or Foolish?

It was getting late, and Mr. McMath had walked a long time. As he reached the town, he felt hungry and tired.

"I will go into that shop to get some bread and maybe a cold drink," he said.

Just then, the shopkeeper came out of the door carrying a large sack on his back.

"What have you got there, my good man?" asked Mr. McMath.

"Apples," said the shopkeeper. "A whole sack of apples for my pigs."

148

"Think of that!" said Mr. McMath.
"My wife would really like a sack of apples.
Why, last winter we had only one apple
in the house. My wife said that one apple
was better than nothing. But even so,
I wish she could have a whole sack of apples."

"Well, my pigs can wait," said the shopkeeper.
"What will you give me for these apples?"

"Will this goose do?"
asked Mr. McMath, who was tired
of carrying the heavy goose
under his arm.

The shopkeeper knew
that goose feathers
would make a nice, soft bed.
So he said, "Fine! Let's trade."

Now some farmers were sitting at a table in the shop, and they heard Mr. McMath talking to the shopkeeper. They wanted him to tell the whole story.

So Mr. McMath told how he had traded his horse for a cow, the cow for a sheep, and the sheep for a goose with fine feathers.

The farmers already knew what he had done with the goose. But Mr. McMath went on with his story, telling how he had traded the goose for a sack of apples.

"Ho, ho!" cried one of the farmers.
"That was a foolish thing to do.
I'll bet your wife will give you trouble
in trade for those apples."

"Not at all," said Mr. McMath. "She will give
me a kiss and say that I did the right thing."

"I'll bet she won't," laughed the farmer.
"I'd even be willing to bet this bag
of silver dollars against your sack of apples."

"Very well, then," said Mr. McMath.
"Come home with me and see for yourself."

So off they went
to take the apples
to Mrs. McMath
and to see
what she would say.

As Mr. McMath walked into the house,
he called out, "Wife, I traded our horse
for a cow."

"How nice!" she cried. "Now we can have
fresh, rich milk to drink every morning."

"Yes, but then I traded the cow for a sheep,"
he said.

"You do have the best ideas!"
answered his wife.
"A sheep will not eat as much grass as a cow."

"Next I traded the sheep for a goose,"
said Mr. McMath.

"Maybe that is better, after all,"
said his wife. "We have not had a fat goose
in years. And we can use the feathers
for a feather bed. You always think
of something to please me!"

"Last of all, I traded the goose
for a whole sack of apples," said Mr. McMath.
"How did you know that I needed apples?"
asked the happy wife. "While you were away,
I wanted to make a pie to surprise you.
But I had no apples to put in it."
And with that, she gave Mr. McMath a big kiss.

The farmer who had made the bet held out
the bag of silver dollars. "You win," he said.
"Your wife gave you a kiss
instead of a lot of trouble."

Mrs. McMath smiled when she saw
the silver dollars. "What a good man I have!"
she said. "And what a good man does
is always right."

Was the last trade wise or foolish?

How to Tell a Tiger

People who know tigers
    Very very well
All agree that tigers
    Are not hard to tell.
The way to tell a tiger is
    With lots of room to spare.
Don't try telling them up close
    Or we may not find you there.

John Ciardi

The Jackal and the Tiger

A large tiger is walking along a path through the woods. He is talking to himself and to anyone who might be listening.

TIGER: Just look at me! Am I not wonderful?

Has there ever been a tiger

with such bright colors?

Or with fur as soft as this?

Or a tail so long and beautiful?

And listen to my voice when I roar!

The tiger roars and goes on talking.

TIGER: When I roar, the elephants stand still.

And the monkeys climb higher in the trees.

The tiger sees a trap with a piece
of meat in it. He walks into the trap
to get the meat. The door of the trap
shuts quickly. Now the silly tiger
is trapped.

TIGER: Help! Help! Will someone help me?
I'm sure someone out there can hear me.

He roars two or three times.
The elephants and the monkeys hear
the tiger, but they don't move.
Suddenly the tiger sees a jackal
coming down the path toward him.

TIGER: Jackal! Jackal! Help me. I stepped
in here to get a piece of meat,
and I'm trapped!

JACKAL: So I see.

TIGER: Will you help me? It would be easy
for you to open the door and set me free.

JACKAL: It would be easy for me to help you.
But if I do, you will eat me.

TIGER: What a silly thing to say!
I've already had a piece of meat.

JACKAL: Then you will not eat me?

TIGER: No. Besides, you're not fat enough.

JACKAL: Then I'll open the door.

The jackal lifts the door of the trap.
The tiger jumps on him and holds him
down with his paw.

TIGER: Ah, at last I have you! I'm so hungry
I will eat you, even if there isn't
much meat on your bones.

JACKAL: But, Tiger, Tiger!
You said you wouldn't eat me.

TIGER: You silly jackal! That piece of meat
wasn't enough for a really hungry tiger.
Now be quiet so I can eat.

JACKAL: Please, Tiger, wait! Will you give me
a chance to ask a question?

TIGER: Ask your question. And be quick.

I am VERY hungry.

JACKAL: Let me walk down this path.

I will ask the first three I meet

the following question: 'Is it fair

for the tiger to eat me?'

If they all say 'Yes,'

then I will let you eat me.

But if one of them should say 'No,'

you must let me go.

TIGER: That's a silly question!

I know they will all say 'Yes.'

But go and find out for yourself.

JACKAL: Oh, thank you, Tiger! Thank you so much.

The jackal walks away into the woods.
Soon he comes to a large tree
with many branches.

JACKAL: Oh, Tree, I hope you can help me.

I'm in a lot of trouble.

TREE: I'm sorry you are in trouble.

But you aren't the only one.

I have so much trouble

I am sad all the way

down to my roots.

JACKAL: Listen, Tree. While I was walking
down this path, I came upon a tiger
who was caught in a trap. I let him out,
and now he wants to eat me.
Do you think that's fair?

TREE: Well, just look at me. I grew leaves
on my branches to keep the hot sun
off those who pass by or stop to rest.
Then they take my branches for firewood.
So I have troubles, too.
Go and let the tiger eat you.

JACKAL: Not yet.

The jackal starts down the path again.
An ox pulling a heavy load passes by.

JACKAL: I say there, Ox, may I ask you
a question? I hope you can help me.

OX: What is your question, Jackal?

JACKAL: I was walking along this path
when I came across a wild tiger who was
caught in a trap. So I let him out.
And now he wants to eat me.
Don't you think it would be wrong
for him to eat me?

OX: Well, Jackal, I hope you don't think
you are the only one who has trouble.
All day long I have to pull heavy loads
for a farmer. He never gives me a chance
to rest, and I'm always tired.
No, I don't feel sorry for you.
Go and let the tiger eat you.

JACKAL: Not yet.

The jackal goes down the path.
Soon he comes to a wide road.

JACKAL: Oh, Road, can you save me?

ROAD: Maybe. What's wrong?

JACKAL: Not long ago I found a wild tiger
caught in a trap, and I let him out.
As soon as he was out, he wanted
to eat me. Do you think that's fair?

ROAD: Is that why you are sad? Well, look at me.
I have my troubles, too.
I give people a wide path to walk on.
They carry their heavy loads over me
and don't even bother to thank me.
So, how can I get excited about a tiger
who may not be fair? For all I care,
you can go back and let the tiger eat you.

JACKAL: Oh, me! Oh, my! I can't find anyone
who wants to save me.

The jackal starts back toward the tiger.
On the way he meets a fox.

FOX: Why are you so sad, Jackal?
JACKAL: I was trying to be kind to the tiger,
and I let him out of a trap.
As soon as he was out, he wanted
to eat me. During my walk down this path,
I asked the tree, the ox, and the road
if they think the tiger is fair.
But they don't seem to care what happens
to me. All of them told me to go back
and let the tiger eat me.
Now do you see why I am sad?

FOX: I don't think I understand.
I'm sorry, but your story is not clear.
Suppose I go with you to find the tiger.
I'll ask him some questions, and maybe
I can get the story straight in my mind.

*The fox and the jackal walk back
to the place where the tiger is waiting.*

TIGER: Well, I'm glad you are back. It's noon
and I'm hungry. I want to eat now!
JACKAL: In a minute, Tiger. First the fox
wants to ask you a question.

168

FOX: I can't seem to understand
the jackal's story. Will you please
tell me what this is all about,
so that it will be clear in my mind?

TIGER: There's not much to tell. I stepped
into a trap to get a piece of meat,
and I got caught.

FOX: Is that the trap?

TIGER: Yes.

FOX: What happened next?

TIGER: Jackal came by and was kind enough
to let me out of the trap.

FOX: And now you want to thank him
for his kindness?

TIGER: Well, not really. I want to eat him.
He doesn't have much meat on his bones,
but I am VERY hungry.

FOX: I still don't understand. Help me get
the story straight. I believe you said
that the jackal was in the trap.
You let him out so you could eat him.
But now he won't say 'Thank you.'

TIGER: No, no, no! You have it all wrong!
I was the one in the trap. See? Like this!

The tiger jumps into the empty trap.
The fox quickly shuts the door.

TIGER: I was in the trap. Jackal came along
and let me out. Do you understand?

This time the jackal does not move
toward the trapdoor.

171

FOX: Now I see what happened.
It's clear in my mind.

TIGER: Let me out! Let me out!

The jackal begins to laugh.

TIGER: Oh, Jackal, let me out of here.
Right now! Throw open the door
so I'll be able to get out!

The jackal is still laughing.

JACKAL: Now I understand, Fox. I believe
you really wanted to save me.
So you thought of a clever trick
to play on the tiger. Let me thank you.

FOX: Think nothing of it. I was happy to do it.

The jackal and the fox walk away together.

TIGER: Let me out! Let me out! Help! Help!

This time the elephants do not stand still. The monkeys do not climb higher in the trees. Instead they all make lots of happy noises.

TIGER: Won't anyone help a poor hungry tiger?

Would you help the tiger?

173

The Fisherman and His Wife

There was once a poor fisherman who lived with his wife in a little hut not far from the sea. Almost every day, right after breakfast, the fisherman went down to the sea to catch fish.

One day as he was fishing and looking
into the clear, blue water, he saw a large fish
on the end of his line. The fish was so big
that it took the fisherman's line deep down
into the water.

The waves were high, and the fisherman
had trouble pulling in his line.
It was almost noon before he had the fish
out of the water.

To the man's surprise the fish cried out:

"Fisherman, fisherman, listen to me.
Let me go free, let me go free.
I'm not a real fish, but a prince, you see.
If you pull me out, what good will I be?"

"A talking fish!" said the fisherman.
"Maybe I will let you go. A fish who talks
might not be good to eat."
So he took the fish off the line
and threw it back into the highest wave.
Soon the fish was deep down in the sea.
Then the fisherman went home
to his wife in the hut.

"Well, husband," called the wife
in a cross voice. "Have you caught
anything today?"

"Not to eat," he answered.
"But you'll never guess what I did catch.
A fish that talks! He said he was really
a prince, so I threw him back into the sea."

"Oh, no!" cried his wife.

"Not until you made a wish, I hope."

"I didn't make a wish," said the husband. "What would I wish for?"

"What!" shouted the angry wife. "It's easy to make a wish. You might have asked for something useful. I'm tired of this old, gray hut. Go back and wish for a house. The talking fish just might give it to us."

The man went back and stood at the edge
of the sea. He called:

"Oh, prince of the sea, come listen to me.
For Alice, my wife, who upsets my life,
Has sent me to ask a wish of thee."

The fish poked his head out of a high wave
and asked, "Now then, what does she want?"
"Oh," said the man. "My wife says
I should have asked for something
when I caught you.
She does not want to live
in the hut any longer,
and would like to have a house."
"Go home!" ordered the fish.
"She already has her wish."

So the fisherman went home and found,
instead of the hut, a house with a garden.
And there, sitting in the kitchen, was his wife.

"Isn't this house better than the old,
gray hut?" she asked.

"Yes, it is," said her husband.
"Now we should be happy the rest of our days."

"I wonder," answered his wife.

Wishes! Wishes! Wishes!

Then one morning the wife said, "This house
is really too small. I think the fish
could give us a larger house. I would like
to live in a castle. Go to your fish
and ask him for a castle."

"Oh, my dear wife!" said the husband.
"This house is big enough. Why would we want
to live in a castle?"

"Go along," said the wife. "The fish
might just as well give it to us. Do as I say!"

The man did not want to go, and he said
to himself, "It's not the right thing to do."
But he went anyway.

When he reached the edge of the sea,
he stood there and shouted:

"Oh, prince of the sea, come listen to me.
For Alice, my wife, who upsets my life,
Has sent me to ask a wish of thee."

Suddenly the fish popped up
above the high wave and asked, "Now then,
what does she want?"

"She wants to live in a castle,"
answered the fisherman.

"Go home!" called the fish. "Your wife
is standing at the castle door."

And with that he was gone.

The fisherman walked along the same path
he had followed before. But the house was gone.
In its place stood a great stone castle,
and standing on the steps was his wife.

She took him by the hand and said,
"Come. Let's go inside."

With that, he followed her
through the whole castle.
At last he said, "This castle
is all we could ever want.
We should be happy here
the rest of our lives."

"We will see about that,"
said the wife.

The next morning the wife was standing
on the balcony. She looked down and saw
the beautiful countryside.

"Husband!" she called as she pointed
to the land below. "If you could be King
over all of that, think how happy we would be.
Go to your fish and tell him you want
to be King."

"But I don't want to be King,"
answered her husband.

"Very well," said his wife as she pointed
toward the sea. "If you won't be King,
I will be Queen. Go at once to the fish.
I must be Queen!"

The fisherman didn't want to go.
And yet he went, just to please his wife.
When he reached the sea, he called:

"Oh, prince of the sea, come listen to me.
  For Alice, my wife, who upsets my life,
  Has sent me to ask a wish of thee."

The fish popped up above the waves
and asked, "Now then, what does your wife
want this time?"

"Oh, dear!" said the fisherman.
"She wants to be Queen."

"Go home," the fish told him.
"She is already a queen."

So the man went back.
Where the castle had been,
he found a beautiful palace.
It was made of silver and gold.

As the fisherman passed
through the gates of the palace,
he saw his wife sitting
on a throne. Upon her head
was a golden crown.

The fisherman walked
toward the throne and said,
"Well, Wife, so you are Queen.
Now there is nothing more
to ask for."

"Time will tell," said his wife.

With that, she went to bed.
But she could not sleep,
because she kept thinking
of what she would like
to have next.

In the morning, as she sat watching the sun, she said, "Oh, I know! What if I could make the sun and moon to shine?"

"Husband!" she called. "Get up and go to your fish. Tell him I want power over the sun and moon."

"Oh, Wife! No!" he cried. "Don't be foolish. The fish cannot do that."

"And why not?" she asked. "All I want now is power over the sun and moon. I think it would be nice to have light or dark whenever I wished. If I had that kind of power, I would be happy for the rest of my days."

When the fisherman just stood there,
his wife grew angry. She was so angry
that the heavy crown fell off her head.

"Do as I say!" she ordered. "Go speak
to the talking fish!"

The fisherman didn't want to go.
But after all, his wife was Queen.

When he reached the sea, he cried out:

"Oh, prince of the sea, come listen to me.
For Alice, my wife, who upsets my life,
Has sent me to ask a wish of thee."

The fish poked his head above a wave
and asked, "Well, what now?"

"Oh dear!" said the man. "My wife
wants power over the sun and the moon."

"Go home with you," said the fish.
"You will find her in the old hut.
Just as before."

And there you will find the fisherman
and his foolish wife, even now.

Tikki Tikki Tembo

Once upon a time, long, long ago,
all fathers and mothers in China
gave their first born sons great long names.

But second born sons were given names
that were not long at all.

In a small village in China lived a mother
who had two sons. Her second born son
she called Chang, which means
"little or nothing."

But her first born son she called
Tikki tikki tembo-no sa rembo, which means
"most wonderful thing in the whole wide world."

Every morning the mother went to wash
clothes in a river near the village.
Her two young sons always went with her.

On the bank of the river was an old well.

Every day the mother would say to her sons,
"Don't go near the well. It is deep
and you will surely fall in."

But the young boys did not always mind
their mother. One day as they were playing
on the bank of the river near the well,
Chang fell in.

Tikki tikki tembo-no sa rembo ran as fast
as his little legs could carry him.

When he reached his mother, he shouted,
"Good Mother, my brother Chang has fallen
into the well!"

"The noise of the water is loud
in this place," said the mother.
"And I cannot hear you."

Tikki tikki tembo-no sa rembo
shouted in a louder voice,
"Oh Great and Good Mother,
Chang has fallen into the well!"

"That boy is more trouble!"
answered the mother.
"Run to the village and get
the Old Man with the Ladder
to fish him out."

Tikki tikki tembo-no sa rembo ran as fast
as his little legs could carry him.
When he reached the Old Man with the Ladder,
he said, "Chang, my brother, has fallen
into the well. Will you come and fish him out?"

"So!" said the Old Man with the Ladder.
"Chang has fallen into the well.
Come. Lead me to him."

The Old Man ran as fast as his old legs
could carry him. Then step over step,
step over step, he went down into the well.

He picked up little Chang
and step over step, step over step,
brought him out of the well.

The Old Man pumped water out of Chang
and pushed air into him. He pumped the water
out of him and pushed the air into him.

Soon Chang was just as good as ever.
Then the Old Man slowly carried his ladder
back to the village.

Now for a long time, the young boys did not
go near the well. But on the Day of Magic Kites,
they went to sit on the bank of the river
to eat their rice cakes. As they ate,
they watched the beautiful kites
flying high above them in the clear, blue sky.

When they had finished eating the rice cakes,
they walked along the top of the well.
Now that was not a good idea,
because Tikki tikki tembo-no sa rembo fell in.

Chang ran as fast as he could.

When he reached his mother, he said,

"Oh, Good Mother, Tikki tikki tembo-no sa rembo

has fallen into the well!"

"Speak up, child," said the mother.

"The noise of the water is so loud

I cannot hear you."

"Good Mother, Great Mother,

your first born son,

Tikki tikki tembo-no sa rembo,

has fallen into the well!"

shouted Chang.

"Tiresome child,

what are you trying to say?"

asked the mother.

"Good Mother, listen to me!" said Chang, stopping to rest his voice.

"Tikki no sa rembo has fallen into the well!"

"Tiresome boy!" said his mother.

"Some magic hides in your mouth and plays tricks with your voice. I have often told you to speak your brother's wonderful name with great care."

Chang had run so hard and so fast that his voice was almost as tired as his short legs. He didn't think he could say one more word.

Then he remembered his poor brother in the deep well.

Chang looked at his mother.
Then slowly, very slowly he said,
"Tikki tikki tembo-no sa rembo
has fallen into the well!"

"Oh no, not my first born son!"
said his mother. "Run quickly!
Tell the Old Man with the Ladder
that your brother has fallen
into the well."

So Chang ran as fast
as his short legs could carry him
to the Old Man with the Ladder.

There under a tree sat the Old Man
with a cricket cage in his lap.
He was dreaming as he listened
to the music of the crickets.

"Old Man, Old Man!" shouted Chang.
"Come right away! Tikki tikki tembo-no sa rembo
has fallen into the well!"

But the Old Man said nothing. Chang wasn't
sure what he should do. Then, as tired
as he was, he shouted again, "Old Man,
my brother Tikki tikki tembo-no sa rembo
has fallen into the well."

"Be still, my child,"
said the Old Man in an angry voice.
"Go away! I want to listen
to the music of my crickets.
I want to finish my dream
about golden fireflies
that make the night
as bright as day."

By now Chang was almost ready to cry.
How could he say that great long name again?
He wished his brother had a short name
like Chang.

"Please, Old Man with the Ladder, please help
my poor brother out of the well," he said.

"So!" said the Old Man.
"Your mother's wonderful number-one son
has fallen into the well, has he?"

The Old Man with the Ladder
took the cricket cage from his lap
and put it on the ground.
Then he hurried as fast
as his old legs could carry him
to the well.

Step over step, step over step,
he went down inside the well.
And step over step, step over step,
he brought Tikki tikki tembo-no sa rembo out.

The Old Man pumped water out of him
and pushed air into him. He pumped the water
out of him and pushed the air into him.

But Tikki tikki tembo-no sa rembo had been
in the water a long, long time.
And the water had been in him a long time, too.
All because of his great long name.

Many days and nights went by
before Tikki tikki tembo-no sa rembo
was quite the same again.

And from that day to this,
all Chinese mothers and fathers
have thought it wise to give their children
little short names instead of great long names.

Finding a Way

Kay Keeps a Secret

Kay Bridges planned to be at school early this morning. Her teacher, Mr. Banks, and some of the other girls and boys would be early, too.

Her class was getting ready to act out a school play. All during the last week Kay had been reading her part in the play. This morning she was going to act out her part.

Each child would also have a chance to talk about the clothes to wear in the play.

204

Kay's mom and dad had already gone to work,
so Kay ate breakfast by herself. Then she
got ready for school and put on her heavy coat.

Taking a quick look at the clock,
she went outside and carefully locked
the front door behind her.

As Kay walked along, her shoes made
a funny crunch-crunch sound on the icy sidewalk.
She passed houses where the lights were still on,
and shops that were not yet open.

Kay heard a motor running as she got close
to a factory. Then she saw a large truck
standing near the factory garage.
The truck was backed up right in front
of the garage doors, ready to be loaded.

The noise of the motor grew louder
as Kay reached the garage, but the truck
had not moved. The front of the truck
was almost covered with ice and snow.

Suddenly Kay stopped. She thought
she could see the driver's head
resting against one of the truck windows.
He wasn't moving! Somehow Kay felt sure
he wasn't sleeping, either. Something was wrong!
Why did the driver look so still?

Kay was afraid. Suppose the driver
was either sick or dead? What should she do?
There was no one else to help.
Many people in that part of the city
were just getting up or were already at work.

Kay went over to the door of the truck
and knocked lightly. The man did not move.
She knocked on the window as hard as she could.
Nothing happened. She tried to open the door.
It was locked! All during this time
the motor kept running.

Kay ran down the block toward the corner.
Then, watching carefully,
she crossed the wide street.

Would anyone be in the newsstand this early? If no one was there, Kay would have to look for help somewhere else.

Maybe she would have to knock on the doors of some apartments until she found help.

Just then Kay saw Mr. Singer carrying the morning papers to the newsstand.

"Hurry, Mr. Singer!" she cried. "Something is wrong. There's a man locked in a truck. When I knocked on the door, he didn't move. He is either hurt, or sick, or—"

Kay was afraid to say that the man might even be dead.

Mr. Singer asked Kay where the truck was.
Then he called the police on the telephone.
He told them Kay's story about the driver.
The police said they would come right away.

Kay began to feel better. She knew
she had done all she could,
so she went straight to school.

Kay reached school about the same time
as her friends. She had made up her mind
not to say anything about what had happened.
She was so busy all day that she even forgot
about the truck driver.

A Day to Remember

That evening after supper, Kay's dad
read a newspaper story out loud.
It told about a man named Jack Green,
who had driven to a factory early that morning.
He hadn't been able to load his truck,
because the factory wasn't open yet.
To keep warm, he had left the motor running.
The police found Mr. Green and broke
into his truck just in time to save his life.

The newspaper said that a young girl
had told Mr. Singer about the driver. But no one,
not even Mr. Singer, knew who the girl was.

Kay had a strange feeling as she listened.
Something kept her from saying that she was
the girl who had helped save Mr. Green's life.

She went into the living room and sat down
to watch TV, just as if it were any other evening.

Two weeks passed and Kay forgot
about Jack Green. Then one day after lunch,
her teacher said that some people
would be coming to visit.

Soon there was a knock on the door.
Mr. Banks opened it and stepped back
to let three men come
into the room.

One of the men had a small box in his hand.
He walked to the front of the room and said,
"Boys and girls, you have a very helpful
young lady in your class. You can be proud
of her."

He smiled at the class and said,
"One morning she saved my life,
but didn't bother to tell anyone her name.
I didn't know who she was until yesterday.
The man at the newsstand remembered
her name and called me."

Kay felt like hiding her head.
She hadn't wanted anyone
to know what she had done
to help the truck driver.

Then she heard, "Kay Bridges,
will you come up here
so I can thank you?"

The children were surprised.
Slowly, Kay got to her feet.
Her teacher smiled at her.
He didn't look surprised at all.
He had known all the time why the men
were coming to visit the class.

Kay went to the front of the room.
As she passed the other boys and girls,
she wondered what they were thinking.

"This is for you, Kay," said Mr. Green.
"I'm happy that I can be here to give you
this present. I hope you like it."

Kay opened a box.

Inside, she found a beautiful ring!

Before she had a chance to say anything, one of the other men said, "I am Mr. Powers from the factory. I have something for you, too. It's from the men who work with Mr. Green. We all want to thank you. We have put one hundred dollars in the bank in your name."

Kay couldn't believe her ears.

"We're all proud of you, Kay," said her teacher. "Now a man from the newspaper wants to take your picture with Mr. Green."

That evening at supper Kay told Mom and Dad
the whole story. She showed them her ring.
They kissed her and told her how proud
they were because she was such a brave girl.

"Just look at this!" said Mom.
"We could hardly wait to show you."

She held up the newspaper and right there
on the front page was Kay's picture!

What a wonderful day it had been.
Kay wouldn't forget it as long as she lived.

City

In the morning the city
Spreads its wings
Making a song
In stone that sings.

In the evening the city
Goes to bed
Hanging lights
About its head.

Langston Hughes

217

Help in the Night

218

Bill May dropped his school books
on a chair, gave his mother a kiss,
and reached for a piece of cake.

"The ice is good and hard," he said.
"I think I'll go out and skate for a while
before supper."

His mother looked up from the apple pie
she was making. "It might be nice
if you would spend some time playing cards
with your brother," she said.
"It would mean a lot to him."

"Oh, Mom," cried Bill. "I'm sick of cards.
All I've done the last few weeks is play
with Jimmy."

He dropped his skates as he said,
"But I suppose I'll have to."

"I didn't say you had to,"
said Mrs. May quietly.

Bill helped himself to another piece
of cake and headed for the dining room.
Jimmy was on the daybed watching TV.
Poor kid! He had been sick for such
a long time. Bill couldn't help feeling sad
when he looked over at his brother.

"Boy, am I glad you're home," said Jimmy.
"I thought the school bus would never
get here."

Bill thought about Jimmy and how much
of the time he had to be alone each day.
There were no close neighbors or friends
out in the country where the May family lived.
Mom was often busy working around the house.
She didn't have very much time left
to spend with Jimmy.

Bill knew that being sick and spending
so much time alone wasn't much fun.
So he tried to put the thought of skating
out of his mind for the time being.

"How about playing a game
of cards?" he asked.

"OK," said Jimmy. "The cards
are over there on the piano."

Bill walked over to the piano.

He picked up the cards and turned around.

Then he saw a sad look on Jimmy's face.

"What's wrong?" asked Bill.
"Don't you want to play cards?"

"I guess you're tired of card games,"
answered his brother. "Let's do something
you want to do for a change."

Bill thought for a minute.

"OK," he said. "I've always wanted to learn
the Morse code. Maybe we can learn it together.
Want to do that for a change?"

Jimmy was excited. "Hey, that sounds great.
Then we can tap out secrets to each other
and no one else will know what we're saying!"

Bill dropped the cards and went to hunt
for the code handbook he had brought from camp.

When he came back, he said to Jimmy,
"We have lots to learn. But soon we should
be able to put short taps and long taps
together to make words."

As he spoke, Bill tapped on the table
with the end of a ball-point pen.

By suppertime both of the boys
were tapping out "hello" to each other
with the pen.

Bill and Jimmy worked until bedtime.

Then Mrs. May came into the room.

She reached for the pen and made

nine short taps on the table before she spoke.

"That sound means nine o'clock,"

she laughed. "And nine o'clock means bedtime."

Later, when Mrs. May said goodnight to Bill,

she thanked him for being so kind to Jimmy.

"I'm glad I changed my mind

about going skating," said Bill.

"Learning the Morse code is a lot more fun

than I had thought it would be.

Besides, when I go back to camp this summer,

I can teach it to the other boys."

In the days that followed, Bill and Jimmy

worked as a team learning how to use

the Morse code.

One evening Mr. May brought home a strange

looking surprise. It was a small block of wood

that had a buzzer on it.

"Will this be useful while you're learning the Morse code?" he asked.

"It sure will!" cried Bill, as he dropped his pen into his shirt pocket. "Using a buzzer to buzz out the words will work much better than tapping them out with a ball-point pen."

Trouble in the Fog

All through the long winter the boys used the buzzer to tell each other things in code. When spring came, Jimmy began feeling better and went back to school.

One spring evening Mr. May asked, "Bill, how would you like to drive to town with me? I believe it's about time for us to visit your grandmother again. A visit with you might make her feel better."

Bill thought it would be more fun to watch TV instead. But he knew his dad would like to have him along on the drive into town.

"OK, I'll go," he said, as he went into the bedroom to change his shirt.

"Do you think you should go tonight?"
asked Mrs. May, looking out the window.
"There seems to be quite a bit of fog.
If the fog gets heavy, you'll have a hard time
seeing the road."

"Don't worry," answered Mr. May.
"I don't think the fog will bother us."

But after he and Bill had gone
a mile or two, the fog got heavier.

"Maybe we'd better go back," said Mr. May.
"The fog is so heavy I can hardly see the road."

He turned around and headed toward home.
They drove along without talking.
Dad didn't want to worry Bill.
And Bill didn't want Dad to think
he was afraid.

Bill rolled down the window.
It was hard to see the road signs
or anything else
through the heavy fog.

As they drove over a bridge,
Bill saw a neighbor's mailbox.
Now he knew they were only a half mile
from home.

"Careful, Dad!" he called.
"You're too far over on the side of the road!"

Suddenly a wild fox ran out of the fog,
right in front of the car.
As Mr. May tried to miss the fox,
he drove off the road, straight into a tree.

A large branch broke off and fell on the car.
Bill's door was blocked by the branch.

Bill tried to move, but his left leg hurt.
He looked at his dad. He wasn't moving at all!
Mr. May had been knocked out when he drove
into the tree.

Bill knew that he had to get help in a hurry.
But how? He would never be able to walk
the rest of the way home because of his leg.
Besides, the car door was blocked by the branch.
He couldn't open it. What could he do?

Then Bill thought of the horn. The motor
had stopped running when the car hit the tree.
Was the horn dead? If it wasn't,
maybe he could use it to get help.

He reached over and pushed on the horn
as hard as he could. It worked!
A loud sound cut through the heavy fog.

Bill began to tap for help, using the code.
Over and over he tapped the horn
until his fingers hurt. What if no one heard?
What would happen to Dad if no one came?
Bill kept on tapping.

At home, Jimmy and his mother were
in the dining room playing a game.
   "Listen!" cried Jimmy.
"Listen to that sound. Does someone want help?
Could it be Bill? Do you suppose he and Dad
are in some kind of trouble?"

Mrs. May called the police.
"Someone needs help," she said.
"Could you send a man to see what's wrong?"

In a short time the police found Bill
and Mr. May. They helped Bill and his dad
out of the car and drove them home
in the police car.

The S O S call that Bill had tapped
out on the horn had brought help in time.
Mr. May had been knocked out for a while,
but before long he was all right.

In the weeks that followed,
Bill's leg got better. He thought a lot
about what had happened. He knew that at first
he hadn't really wanted to spend much time
with his little brother.

What if they hadn't learned the Morse code?
What if Dad hadn't brought the buzzer home?
And what if Dad had been all alone
in the car that night?

"We were lucky, Mom," he said. "Just lucky."

"Yes, I suppose you were," said Mrs. May.
"But luck doesn't just happen.
Most of the time we bring about our own luck."

Bill smiled. He knew that in her own way
his mother was saying that she was proud of him.

Space Secrets

See if you can read this letter code.

BRINGHELPRIGHTAWAY

Look carefully at the letters,
and you will see four words.
But there are no spaces between them.
If you put spaces in the right places,
the words will be easy to read.

BRING HELP RIGHT AWAY

Here is another way to code the letters:

BRI NGH ELP RIG HTA WAY

Now see if you can work out
these other "space secrets." Good luck!

1. HIDEBEHINDTHEHOUSE

2. LOO KIN THE GAR AGE

3. TA PI FY OU AR ER EA DY

Fog

The fog comes
on little cat feet.

It sits looking
over harbor and city
on silent haunches
and then, moves on.

Carl Sandburg

Dark Sky for Ana

Today was the day Mr. Gomez was coming to buy a horse. Which one would he pick?

Ana had thought about nothing else for days. She knew her dad had to sell one of the horses she loved so much.

She was afraid Dad would sell Dark Sky, and she wanted to keep him for herself. So Ana was worried.

As Ana stood by the fence, she watched three young horses circle around the pasture. One horse could run faster and kick higher than the others. He had a shiny black coat and was named Dark Sky.

During the last few weeks Ana and Dark Sky had become good friends.

Sometimes when Ana stood by the fence,
he would kick up his feet and come running
across the pasture toward her.
Quite often she would give him an apple.

    And once in a while, Dark Sky
would let Ana brush his beautiful shiny coat.
While she brushed, she always spoke softly
to him. Dark Sky would point his ears
toward her and listen to her voice.

This very noon, as Ana was eating lunch,
her mother had said, "You're worrying
about Dark Sky again, aren't you?
You might as well forget him, dear. Dad says
you're too young to train your own horse."

"But, Mom, I've always dreamed of having
a horse of my own to train," answered Ana.
"Besides, I can ride and rope
as well as my brothers. If either of them
wanted Dark Sky, I bet Dad wouldn't say no."

"Just being able to ride and rope
isn't enough," said her mother.
"You have to be strong to train a horse
like Dark Sky. Dad is afraid
he might kick you or throw you."

"That's not fair!" cried Ana.
"It's how carefully you train a horse
that really counts, not how strong you are."

"I know how you must feel, dear,"
answered her mother.
"But I don't believe Dad will change his mind."

Putting an apple in her shirt pocket,
Ana hurried outside. She walked over
to the pasture and stood by the fence.

Black Magic and Silver Dollar
were quietly chewing the new spring grass.
But not Dark Sky. He seemed excited
as he circled about inside the fence.

How Ana loved to watch him!
He held his proud head high in the air
and kicked his strong legs.

Ana wished Dad would change his mind!
She would give anything, she thought,
for a chance to train Dark Sky. But she felt
that her wish to train him was just a dream.

As Ana stood watching the horses,
a covered truck drove up the driveway.
It was Mr. Gomez!

Dad hurried over to the truck,
and the men began talking together.
Ana just knew they were talking about the horses,
because Mr. Gomez pointed toward the pasture.
Was he pointing to Dark Sky?

Ana really began to worry as the men walked toward the pasture. Mr. Gomez was sure to buy the very horse she liked best.

When Dad unlocked the gate, Ana could see that he was carrying a lead rope.
He walked slowly up to Dark Sky
and started to put the rope around his neck.

What do you think Ana will do now?

A Dream Comes True

Dark Sky did not like to have anything
around his neck. Suddenly he kicked his feet
and began running wildly around the pasture.
He went straight through the open gate
and headed for a field behind the house.

"Where will he go?" wondered Ana.

Dark Sky wouldn't know his way around
the rest of the farm. He had never been out
of the fenced-in pasture before.
Dad had always kept the gate locked.

A minute later Ana heard the horse cry out.
Was Dark Sky in trouble? She was afraid
to even think what might have happened to him.

Ana hurried behind the house.
When she saw the broken cover of the old well,
she knew why Dark Sky had cried out.
He had fallen into the well!

The cover was not strong enough to hold
the young horse. He had broken through the wood
and dropped into the water below.

"Dad! Dad!" shouted Ana.
"Dark Sky has fallen into the old well!"

Looking down over the edge, Ana could see
the horse kicking wildly. "Don't worry,
Dark Sky," she called. "We'll get you out."

By that time Dad and Mr. Gomez had also reached the well.

"Throw a line around Dark Sky's neck!" cried Ana. "Keep his head above the water."

"There's no way we can save him," said Dad in a sad voice. "You know that, don't you?"

"We just have to save him!" cried Ana. "I think I know a way."

Ana ran across the yard toward the new well. She picked up the large hose that carried water to the nearby crops.

As she turned on the powerful pump, the water roared out of the hose. It came out so fast that Ana was knocked to the ground.

Dad and Mr. Gomez ran to help. Together they pulled the big hose to the edge of the old well.

The water was pumped into the well, and slowly, ever so slowly, Dark Sky was lifted up.

It was not long before the water reached
the top of the well and the men were able
to help Dark Sky over the edge. They took
the rope off his neck and he dropped
to the ground.

Dark Sky was afraid, but not hurt.
His legs were too tired to hold him up,
and he lay resting on the grass.

Ana dropped down beside the horse.
"It's OK, Dark Sky," she said.
"You're all right now."

Dad smiled at Ana and said,
"I guess I was wrong."

He turned to Mr. Gomez.
"I can't sell this horse,"
he said. "You'll have to pick
Black Magic or Silver Dollar,
instead of Dark Sky."

Ana couldn't believe her ears. Maybe her dream was going to come true after all.

"Oh, Dad!" she cried in an excited voice. "Do you mean I can have Dark Sky?"

"I'm very proud of the way you used your head to help him," said her dad. "He might be dead if it weren't for you. So I've changed my mind. I'll give you a chance to train Dark Sky. He's your horse now."

Mr. Gomez seemed to understand.

"I'd like to own Dark Sky," he said. "But your quick thinking saved him, Ana. So it's only right that he should belong to you."

Did Ana's dream come true? Why?

The Flat Tire Mystery

Kip Peterson had waited and waited
for summer to come. At last it was here,
and he was spending a few weeks visiting
Grandmother and Grandfather Peterson
in the city.

Living on a farm was fine, but there were
so many different things to do in the city.
Something exciting was always happening.
There were large stores to shop in,
a zoo to visit, and a playground where Kip
could always find someone to play with.

Kip really liked the zoo. It was fun
to watch all the strange animals and birds.
But the zoo didn't have a pet crow like Lucky.

"I'm glad you let me bring
Lucky along," Kip said to Gram.
"He sure misses me when I'm gone."
    Kip opened the door
of the bird's cage and threw in
a handful of corn.
    "Caw, caw," said the crow.
He jumped down and began to peck
at the bright yellow pieces of corn.
    "I'm just sorry Lucky has to stay
locked up in his cage," said Gram.
"That can't be much fun
for a crow who is used to flying
around outside."
    "He can fly around the yard
while I cut the grass," answered Kip.
    "Are you sure he won't fly away?" asked Gram.
"This is a strange place, you know."
    "Don't worry," said Kip. "Lucky is
a very clever bird. He never goes too far away,
and he always comes when I whistle."

Kip opened the door of the cage
as far as it would go. He held out
his hand and whistled. Lucky
flew out and sat on his finger.
Then they went outside together.

First Kip cut the grass
in the front yard, then in the back.

Lucky flew from tree to tree,
hunting for something to eat.
Sometimes he would stop long enough
to peck at the shiny leaves.

Once he even flew over
and sat on top of Gramps' car,
where it stood in the driveway.

"Caw, caw," he cried.
Lucky sounded
as if he were happy
to be free.

251

Just as Kip finished cutting the grass,
Gramps came out the front door.

"Want to ride to the store with me?" he called.

"Sure, Gramps," answered Kip.
"But first let me put Lucky back in his cage."

Gramps pointed to his car and said, "Oh, no!
Look at that! Two flat tires. I must have run over
some glass in the road." He went into the house
to call a man from the garage.

When the garageman had fixed the tires,
he said, "I can't find any glass in your tires.
Looks like somebody let the air out of them."

Gramps looked surprised. Then he spoke to Kip. "You didn't do anything to the tires, did you?"

"I didn't go near the car, Gramps," said Kip. "Besides, I was busy cutting the grass."

"Well, the tires are fixed now," said Gramps. "So that should be the end of our trouble."

But it wasn't the end. When Kip came back after spending the afternoon at the zoo, he found Gramps looking at the car. This time there were three flat tires!

"This isn't funny," he heard Gramps say.

"Some of the neighbor children must be playing tricks," answered Gram.

"Just about all of the children are away at camp," said Gramps.

"All but Jim," said Gram. "But he couldn't have let the air out of the tires. He and Kip were at the zoo all afternoon."

"Well," said Kip. "Somebody's bothering your tires. And I'm going to find out who it is."

So right after lunch the next day,
Kip took Lucky outside. He lay down on the grass
to watch the car while Lucky flew happily about
from tree to tree.

Kip waited. The hot sun made him feel sleepy,
and he closed his eyes. Suddenly he heard
a funny noise. S-ss-sst!

He opened his eyes. He couldn't believe
what he saw! There, right beside the car
was Lucky, pecking at something on the tire.
Each time he pecked, air would whistle out.

"You trickster!" laughed Kip.

"That's no way to get cool."

Gramps laughed, too, when he heard
who had been letting the air out of his tires.

"You were right, Kip," he said.

"That Lucky is a clever crow.

Just too clever, if you ask me."

(Acknowledgments continued from page 2.)

Grosset & Dunlap, Inc., for "The Jackal and the Tiger." Adapted from THE OLD MAN AND THE TIGER by Alvin Tresselt. Copyright © 1965 by Grosset & Dunlap, Inc. Published by Grosset & Dunlap, Inc.

Harcourt Brace Jovanovich, Inc., for the poem "Fog." From CHICAGO POEMS by Carl Sandburg, copyright, 1916, by Holt, Rinehart and Winston, Inc.; copyright, 1944, by Carl Sandburg. Reprinted by permission of Harcourt Brace Jovanovich, Inc.

The Holiday Publishing Company, Inc., for "Kay Keeps a Secret." Adapted from "Moment of Crisis" by Beth Bolling. Reprinted by permission from JACK AND JILL Magazine. Copyright 1971. The Holiday Publishing Company, Inc.

Holt, Rinehart and Winston, Inc., for "Tikki Tikki Tembo." Adaptation of the Holt, Rinehart and Winston edition of TIKKI TIKKI TEMBO retold by Arlene Mosel and illustrated by Blair Lent. Copyright © 1968 by Arlene Mosel. Reprinted by permission of Holt, Rinehart and Winston, Inc.

J. B. Lippincott Company for the poem "How to Tell a Tiger" by John Ciardi. From the book YOU READ TO ME, I'LL READ TO YOU by John Ciardi. Copyright, © 1962, by John Ciardi. Reprinted by permission of the publishers, J. B. Lippincott Company.

J. B. Lippincott Company for "Sing, Sack, Sing." Adapted from "The Earrings" by Pura Belpré. From the book THE TIGER AND THE RABBIT AND OTHER TALES told by Pura Belpré. Copyright 1944, 1946 and © 1965 by Pura Belpré. "The Earrings" has been reprinted as condensed by permission of the publishers, J. B. Lippincott Company.

JACK AND JILL for "Dark Sky for Ana." Adapted from "The Gentle Touch," by E. Lucas and C. Kutac. Adapted by permission from JACK AND JILL Magazine. Copyright 1970. The Saturday Evening Post Company.

McGraw-Hill Book Company for the finger play "Little Timothy Snail." From GAMES TO PLAY WITH THE VERY YOUNG by Elizabeth Matterson. Copyright © 1969 by Elizabeth Matterson. Used with permission of McGraw-Hill Book Co., & Penguin Books Ltd. Published in Great Britain under the title *This Little Puffin*.

HAROLD OBER ASSOCIATES INCORPORATED for the poem "City" by Langston Hughes. From THE LANGSTON HUGHES READER by Langston Hughes. Copyright © 1958 by Langston Hughes. Reprinted by permission of HAROLD OBER ASSOCIATES INCORPORATED.

Review Publishing Company for "Help in the Night." Adapted by permission from "Distress Signal" by Frances B. Watts. From Golden Magazine, Copyright February, 1971, Review Publishing Company; and for "The Flat Tire Mystery." Adapted by permission from "The Flat Tire Mystery," by Carroll S. Karch. From *Child Life*, copyright 1970 by Review Publishing Co., Inc.